I0102722

Let's Do Hunch ™

©Ellen Palestrant 2016/18

Have a Hunch?
Take it to lunch.
Wine it.
Dine it. Listen to it. Woo it.
If you take your hunch to lunch today...
Tomorrow it might take you.

From I TOUCHED A STAR IN MY DREAM LAST NIGHT ©Ellen Palestrant 2016/18

ADDITIONAL READING: for individual participants, groups, book clubs, creativity clubs, and facilitators:

HAVE YOU EVER HAD A HUNCH? The Importance of Creative Thinking by Ellen Palestrant
I TOUCHED A STAR IN MY DREAM LAST NIGHT by Ellen Palestrant
CONVERSATIONS ABOUT CREATIVITY: Art, Writing, Music, Filmmaking, Theatre, Education & The Synergy of Imagination. Interviews by Ellen Palestrant
QUOTES ABOUT CREATIVITY: Writers, artists, scientists, philosophers, share inspirational thoughts. Compiled by Ellen Palestrant

Copyright © 2018 by Ellen Palestrant

First Edition 2018

10 9 8 7 6 5 4 3 2 1

ISBN: 978-0-9998247-2-6

Poems, cover, and interior artwork © 1994, 2005, 2014, 2016, 2018 by Ellen Palestrant

Poems, illustrations, and artwork have appeared in
I Touched a Star in My Dream Last Night by Ellen Palestrant 2005, 2014
Have You Ever Had a Hunch? The Importance of Creative Thinking by Ellen Palestrant 1994, 2005, 2014
The World of Glimpse by Ellen Palestrant 2012
Our Mark—Creatopia also used in the C.A.P.™ method
(Collaborative Artistic Productions) founded by Ellen Palestrant and Dr. Lisa K. Miller 1997

EP Creative Enterprises
www.EllenPalestrant.com

Front Cover Photo: Eric Cosh
Cover and Interior Layout: The Printed Page, Phoenix, AZ

All rights reserved. No part of this publication may be reproduced, stored in, or introduced into a retrieval system, or transmitted in any form, or by any means (electronic, mechanical, photocopying, recording, or otherwise) without the prior written permission of both the copyright owner and the publisher of this book.

Categories: Creativity, Self-Help, Creative Writing, Art, Education, Study & Teaching

List of Activities

©Ellen Palestrant 2016/18

LET'S DO HUNCH™, *the method, is used by individuals, groups, facilitators, book clubs, writers, artists, actors, business people, interior designers, engineers, lawyers—all people who would like to reclaim and develop their creativity potential, and improve their creative thinking skills.*

Activity 1:
Take Your Hunch to Lunch

©Ellen Palestrant 2016/18

Dear Hunch,

You are spontaneously invited to lunch.

Venue: Anywhere.

Time: Anytime

But…

R.S.V.P. Don't Delay Indefinitely

It Might Soon Be… Past Hunchtime!

Hunches and Creativity

So what is a Hunch?

A hunch is your response, your automatic reaction to a stimulus that has not been influenced by logic. It is often accompanied by a feeling of confidence. A hunch is intuition. It feels right even though it has not been preceded by reasoning and has yet to be verbalized. It is a glimpse of something whole that needs to be focused upon and explored *before* it is analyzed, dissected and defined. That hunch or *glimpse of possibility,* needs to be trusted; it contains something of a truth within your grasp, something to which you are trying to give a permanency. Rejection, if necessary, can come later.

Following a Hunch is a Direct Pathway to your Unique Creative Potential!

Give a future to those unexpected hunches; otherwise they might be lost forever…

©Ellen Palestrant 2016/18

Taking your hunch to lunch should be easy, but it's not. Obstacles stand in your way. These destructive, negative controls, which pounce on intuition, ideas, feelings, as soon as they surface and bury them in conformity and insignificance, are the **hunch crunchers**, and they rob you of your potential. In order to free yourself of their influences and enjoy your creativity, you need to identify them and then

CREATE...

AND CREATE...

AND CREATE...

©Ellen Palestrant 2016/18

©Ellen Palestrant 2016/18

1. Can you describe a *hunch*?

2. Do you ever listen to your hunches during your creative process?

©Ellen Palestrant 2016/18

3. Do you trust your hunches?

4. Have you ever had a hunch, followed it, and been proven right? Give an example/s.

©Ellen Palestrant 2016/18

5. Have you ever had a hunch, followed it, and been proven wrong? Give an example/s.

6. Nearly right, perhaps? Give an example/s.

7. Have you ever had a hunch, not followed it, and subsequently wished you had? Give an example/s.

8. Your Personal Hunch Bag for Future Exploration.

Bag your Hunches as they occur.
Some might be ideas worthy of your exploration
NOW

or…sometime in the future:

*9. Circle the words below that best describe your own Creative Processes and
Attitude to Work:*

Abandoned ◇>◇ Adaptable ◇>◇ Ambiguous ◇>◇ Anxious ◇>◇ Attentive
◇>◇ Authentic ◇>◇ Aware ◇>◇ Appreciative ◇>◇ Brave ◇>◇
Cheerful ◇>◇ Childlike ◇>◇ Collaborative ◇>◇ Compromising ◇>◇
Conventional ◇>◇ Conceptual ◇>◇ Confident ◇>◇ Conforming ◇>◇
Commercial ◇>◇ Committed ◇>◇ Completer ◇>◇ Courageous ◇>◇
Controlling ◇>◇ Cowardly ◇>◇ Creative ◇>◇ Critical ◇>◇ Daydreamer
◇>◇ Decisive ◇>◇ Detailed ◇>◇ Disciplined ◇>◇ Divergent Thinker
◇>◇ Dogmatic ◇>◇ Embracer-of-Opportunities ◇>◇ Endurance ◇>◇
Enthusiastic ◇>◇ Experienced ◇>◇ Factual ◇>◇ Fearful ◇>◇ Fervent
◇>◇ Finisher ◇>◇ Focused ◇>◇ Good Values ◇>◇ Gratitude ◇>◇
Happiness ◇>◇ Harmonious ◇>◇ How-to ◇>◇ Honest ◇>◇ Humble
◇>◇ Humorous ◇>◇ Hunch-Follower ◇>◇ Idea-Generator ◇>◇ Impactful
◇>◇ Impulsive ◇>◇ Inattentive ◇>◇ Indecisive ◇>◇ Inspirational ◇>◇
Intimidated ◇>◇ Inauthentic ◇>◇ Inhibited ◇>◇ Innovative ◇>◇
Intuitive ◇>◇ Instinctive ◇>◇ Open ◇>◇ Embracing ◇>◇ Bountiful
◇>◇ Abundant ◇>◇ Generous ◇>◇ Unthreatened ◇>◇ Instruction-
Dependent ◇>◇ Lonely ◇>◇ Motivated ◇>◇ Negative ◇>◇ Joyful
◇>◇ Judgmental ◇>◇ Knowledgeable ◇>◇ Instinctive ◇>◇ Opportunity-
taker ◇>◇ Optimistic ◇>◇ Original ◇>◇ Paranoid ◇>◇ Passionate
◇>◇ Passive ◇>◇ Perceptive ◇>◇ Perfectionist ◇>◇ Persevering ◇>◇
Philosophical ◇>◇ Purposeful ◇>◇ Painful ◇>◇ Positive ◇>◇ Purposeful
◇>◇ Questioning ◇>◇ Religious/Awe-inspired ◇>◇ Spiritual ◇>◇
Repressed ◇>◇ Role Modeled (Real and Illusory) ◇>◇ Self-Conscious ◇>◇
Self-Critical ◇>◇ Self-Expectations ◇>◇ Self-Reliant ◇>◇ self-challenging
◇>◇ Strong ◇>◇ Suppressed ◇>◇ Step-by-Step thinker ◇>◇ Stimulated
◇>◇ Surviving ◇>◇ Silent ◇>◇ Sociable ◇>◇ Solution-Bound ◇>◇
Spiritual ◇>◇ Spontaneous ◇>◇ Team-Player ◇>◇ Tenacious ◇>◇ Trusting
◇>◇ Unconventional ◇>◇ Distrustful ◇>◇ Will-Powered ◇>◇ Other/s...

Activity 2:

Identify the Hunch Crunchers that Stand
In the Way of You and Your Creative Thinking

©Ellen Palestrant 2016/18

THE CENSORSHIP BOARD

STRONGLY ABHORRED...THE INFORMATION IN CIRCULATION...

©Ellen Palestrant 2016/18

Taking your hunch to lunch should be easy, but it's not. Obstacles stand in the way. These barriers judge, condemn, inhibit and drain you of an ability to listen freely to your hunch. They deny you access to an essential route to reaching your creative potential. They compete with your hunch and shout more loudly. These destructive, negative controls, which pounce on intuition, ideas, feelings, as soon as they surface and bury them in conformity and insignificance, are the hunch crunchers, and they rob people of their potential.

These hunch crunchers scream messages suiting their own agendas, and even if much of what they say has value, some recommendations are manipulative and prevent people from becoming self-actualizing. These crunchers function at inferior levels to your hunch, but they are powerful influences.

WARNING!

HUNCH CRUNCHER SPOTTED LURKING IN THE BACK OF YOUR MIND!

Hunch Cruncher

©Ellen Palestrant 2016/18

©Ellen Palestrant 2016/18

1. What are *hunch crunchers*?

2. What situations or which people have *crunched your hunches*?

©Ellen Palestrant 2016/18

Identify Your Hunch Crunchers:

*On a scale of 0 to 10 (0 being not at all; 10 being severe) mark the degree you are affected by the **crunchers** listed below:*

a) **A HURRY-UP CULTURE** *(No time to connect with your inner needs and intuition.)*
1 2 3 4 5 6 7 8 9 10

b) **LACK OF SOLITUDE** *(**No place** to be alone yet aloneness fosters a relationship with creativity)*

1 2 3 4 5 6 7 8 9 10

c) **LACK OF SOLITUDE** *(**No ability** to be alone yet aloneness fosters a relationship with creativity)*

1 2 3 4 5 6 7 8 9 10

d) **INSTRUCTIONAL INTRUSION, EMOTIONAL INTRUSION** *(Ideas and instruction from others can hamper your creativity)*

1 2 3 4 5 6 7 8 9 10

e) **JUDGMENAL INTRUSION** *(The negative effects of expectations, evaluation and criticism.)*

1 2 3 4 5 6 7 8 9 10

f) **REPRESSION** *(Group control of thinking and suppression of new ideas—diversity of thought is essential for creativity.)*

1 2 3 4 5 6 7 8 9 10

g) **INAUTHENTICITY** *(Removal from self, modeling oneself on others, stultifies creative potential.)*

1 2 3 4 5 6 7 8 9 10

©Ellen Palestrant 2016/18

A big hunch cruncher:
FEAR

Fear is realistic. Imaginative, intelligent people fear danger, harm and evil. It is the degree of fear and the related anxieties that can be debilitating and cause natural emotions to become creativity crunchers, limiting the capacity to follow hunches, try new areas, take risks, enjoy life and be productive.

There are times when you need to take risks and there are times when risk-taking is inappropriate. If the water is infested with sharks, don't swim, but if it is filled with ideas to be explored, take the plunge. Risk means venturing where others have not, or staying behind to give more attention when others seemingly move forward. Risk means looking at the known as if it was unknown, and examining the unknown until it is known. Risk can be a stimulant; fear, a cruncher.

©Ellen Palestrant 2016/18

*On a scale of 0 to 10 (0 being not at all; 10 being severe) mark the degree you are affected by **fear**.*

1.	FEAR OF RISK	1 2 3 4 5 6 7 8 9 10
2.	FEAR OF FAILURE	1 2 3 4 5 6 7 8 9 10
3.	FEAR OF SUCCESS	1 2 3 4 5 6 7 8 9 10
4.	FEAR OF BEING DIFFERENT	1 2 3 4 5 6 7 8 9 10
5.	FEAR OF RIDICULE	1 2 3 4 5 6 7 8 9 10
6.	FEAR OF BEING THOUGHT CRAZY	1 2 3 4 5 6 7 8 9 10
7.	FEAR OF BEING ALIENATED	1 2 3 4 5 6 7 8 9 10
8.	FEAR OF BEING MISJUDGED	1 2 3 4 5 6 7 8 9 10
9.	FEAR OF BEING ALONE	1 2 3 4 5 6 7 8 9 10
10.	FEAR OF THE PRESENT (hiding in the past perfect.)	1 2 3 4 5 6 7 8 9 10
11.	FEAR OF NEW POSSIBILITIES	1 2 3 4 5 6 7 8 9 10
12.	FEAR OF ALTERNATIVES	1 2 3 4 5 6 7 8 9 10
13.	FEAR OF AMBIGUITY	1 2 3 4 5 6 7 8 9 10
14.	FEAR OF NEW IDEAS	1 2 3 4 5 6 7 8 9 10
15.	BONDAGE TO THE PAST	1 2 3 4 5 6 7 8 9 10
16.	BONDAGE TO RULES	1 2 3 4 5 6 7 8 9 10
17.	BONDAGE TO REPERTOIRES	1 2 3 4 5 6 7 8 9 10
18.	NEGATIVITY	1 2 3 4 5 6 7 8 9 10
19.	PREMATURE JUDGMENT	1 2 3 4 5 6 7 8 9 10
20.	SOLUTION-BOUND	1 2 3 4 5 6 7 8 9 10
21.	ROLE-BOUND	1 2 3 4 5 6 7 8 9 10

List more of your hunch crunchers:

For example: Procrastination, lack of confidence,

And then...

D-Throne, Overturn & Undermine
Any & All Hunch Crunchers!

And if some remain, sideline them. Don't give them the attention they desire.

©Ellen Palestrant 2016/18

Your Hunch Crunchers have been addressed and your Creative Journey Begins.

Who Knows where it might Lead...

Activity 3:
Prerequisites for Creativity

©Ellen Palestrant 2016/18

©Ellen Palestrant 2016/18

HOW DO YOU CREATE?

Once you have examined the familial, educative, social and political influences on your life and identified your hunch crunchers, it is necessary to take stock of yourself. The final ingredients reside within you. Answer the following questions:

1. How do you approach your projects?

2. Do you take risks in your thinking?

©Ellen Palestrant 2016/18

3. Are you eager to embrace new projects?

4. Are you dedicated?

5. Are you honest with yourself?

©Ellen Palestrant 2016/18

6. Write about your work processes below. (It might help to refer to the chapter on **PREREQUISITES FOR CREATIVITY** from **HAVE YOU EVER HAD A HUNCH?** to help you with the analysis of your approach and attitude to your work.

Activity 4:

Exercises to Develop your Observational Abilities and Increase your Storehouse of Information

©Ellen Palestrant 2016/18

Whether you're a writer, a painter, a filmmaker, a scientist or an educator—whatever your work, whatever your passion—it is important to exercise regularly, your observational skills. Being keenly attuned to external and internal sensory information, supplies you with a rich reservoir (securely lodged in your mind be it in image, auditory, aromatic, tactile or written form) from which you can draw.

When you think critically and examine, investigate, and really look at what you are exposed to, you will not only be a better recorder of the world around you, but also excel at being a retainer of ever-connecting information. You will have an increased ability to assimilate, integrate, shape and harmonize the incoming stimuli rather than just be an individual drawing upon bits of disconnected details going nowhere. You will become a proficient observer when your mind is synchronized with your environment and with the people around you, the details you perceive, the many shades of differences in ever-changing situations—emotional, visual, auditory, tactile, olfactory, gustatory, a mix of it all. You will become a proficient examiner of life.

SO LET'S START EXAMINING...

EXERCISES FOR DEVELOPING SKILLS
FOR PERCEPTIVE OBSERVATION.

(These exercises are good for both individual and group participants.)

A) People: One-On-One Conversation:

Next time you have a conversation with someone, perhaps in your own home, someone else's home or in whatever setting you happen to be, listen to, observe and take note (mentally or written) of...

1. What is being said?

2. What is left unsaid?

3. Does the body language suggest real engagement with the discussion?

4. What do you notice about the placement of hands?

5. What about hand gestures?

6. Is there an authenticity to the conversation?

7. How do you react to the conversation privately and as a participant?

8. How engaged are you in the conversation?

9. How at *home* is the person in your *home* environment?

10. List or make mental notes of subjects discussed.

11. Add more of your perceptions.

B) Group—A Conversation Between A Number of Individuals:

Next time you have a conversation with people, perhaps in your own home, someone else's home or another venue, listen to, observe and take note (mentally or written) of…

1. The seating arrangement (you can draw the seating as well).

2. What is the interaction between them like?

3. Who is the most dominant individual?

4. What about the others?

5. What about you?

6. What is the tone of the conversation—serious, jovial, a mixture of many moods?

7. Is there spontaneous communication between the individuals present?

8. Who controls or primarily determines the conversation?

9. Who contributes the least?

10. Who listens the most attentively?

11. What was your mood like prior to the conversation?

12. What are your reactions during the conversation?

13. Do you or did you feel connected or disconnected to the discussion?

14. Are you a participant or a non-participant observer?

15. List or make mental notes of subjects discussed.

16. How at *home* are the guests in your *home* or whatever environment in which you find yourself?

17. Add more of your perceptions.

C) A Person On Television—Make Notes On:

1. Subject or subjects being discussed.

2. Is this a monologue of an individual person or is it an interview, therefore involving two people?

3. What is being said?

4. What is left unsaid?

5. Does the body language suggest real engagement with what is being discussed?

6. What do you notice about the placement of hands?

7. What about hand gestures?

8. Is there an authenticity to the conversation?

9. How do you react to the conversation and to the participants?

10. How engaged are you in the conversation?

11. Observe voice cadences and background and foreground sounds.

12. How at *home* are the participants in the television environment?

13. Have you learned anything new?

14. Add additional perceptions of your own.

D) A Group of People On Television:

1. Subject or subjects being discussed.

2. Observe the seating arrangement (you can draw it as well).

3. What is the interaction between the participants like?

4. Who is the most dominant individual?

5. What about the others?

6. What about your reactions to the participants' discussions?

7. What is the tone of the conversation, serious, jovial, a mixture of many moods?

8. Is there spontaneity evident in these communication?

9. Who primarily controls or determines the conversation?

10. What do you specifically like and/or dislike about the conversation?

11. How does the conversation affect your mood?

12. Do you feel connected or disconnected to the discussions?

13. Are you a participant or a non-participant listener—that is mentally switched on or quite indifferent or somewhere in between?

14. Observe voice cadences and background and foreground sounds.

15. List or make mental notes of interruptions to and intentional divergences from subjects being discussed.

16. How at home are the participants in the television environment and how authentic does each individual's contribution to the exchange seem to you?

17. Add additional perceptions of your own.

E) Person On the Radio

1. Subject or subjects being discussed.

2. What is being said?

3. What is left unsaid?

4. Do the voice tones and language usage suggest real engagement with what is being discussed?

5. Is there an authenticity to the conversation?

6. How do you react emotionally to the conversation?

7. How engaged are you in the conversation?

8. How at *home* is the person in the broadcast environment?

9. Add more of your perceptions.

F) A Group of People On the Radio:

1. Subject or subjects being discussed.

2. Who are the participants?

3. Observe the emotions of each individual.

4. What is the interaction between them all?

5. Who is the most dominant individual?

6. What about the others?

7. What about you as an audience?

8. What is the tone of the conversation, serious, jovial, a mixture of many moods.

9. Is there a spontaneity to the communication?

10. Control—who primarily determines the conversation?

11. Your reactions—what is your mood?

12. Do you feel connected or disconnected to the discussion?

13. Are you a participant or a non-participant observer?

14. Add more of your perceptions

EXERCISES IN WRITING DIALOGUE:

Exercise 1—Individual Dialogue:

Write your own invented but natural dialogue taking place between *two people*. Their interaction might contain content you wish you had offered in the conversation that you had been observing, or any other conversation you have had in the past. Substitute names—real or invented—for the conversers below. (Extend the exercise if you wish to include more dialogue):

Person A:

Person B:

Person A:

Person B:

Person A:

Person B:

Person A:

Person B:

Person A:

Exercise 2—Group Dialogue:

Write your own invented but natural dialogue taking place between a group of people. Their interaction might contain content you wish you had offered in the conversation that you had been observing, or any other conversation you have had in the past. Substitute names—real or invented—for the conversers below. (Extend the exercise if you wish to include more dialogue):

Person Within Group A:

Person Within Group B:

Person Within Group A:

Person Within Group B:

Person Within Group A:

Person Within Group B:

Person Within Group A:

Person Within Group B:

Person Within Group A:

Person Within Group B:

Person Within Group A:

Exercise 3—Interviewer and Interviewee on Television:

Write your own invented but natural dialogue that takes place between *two people*. Their interaction might contain content that you wish had been offered to you as a viewer by a contributor to the conversation, or by any other interviewer or interviewee to whom you have listened in the past. Substitute names—real or invented—for the conversers below. (Extend the exercise if you wish to include more dialogue):

Interviewer:

Interviewee:

Interviewer:

Interviewee:

Interviewer:

Interviewee:

Interviewer:

Interviewee:

Interviewer:

Interviewee:

Interviewer:

Interviewee:

Exercise 4—Group on Television:

Write your own invented but natural dialogue taking place between a group of people on television. Their interaction might contain content you wish you had offered in the conversation that you had been observing, or any other conversation to which you have listened in the past. Substitute names—real or invented—for the conversers below. (Extend the exercise if you wish to include more dialogue):

Individual:

Individual:

Individual:

Individual:

Indivdual:

Individual:

Individual:

Individual:

Individual:

Individual:

Exercise 5—Radio Interview:

Write your own invented but natural dialogue taking place between *two people*. Their interaction might contain content you wish you had offered in the conversation that you had been observing, or any other conversation you have had in the past. Substitute names—real or invented—for the conversers below. (Extend the exercise if you wish to include more dialogue):

Interviewer:

Interviewee:

Interviewer:

Interviewee:

Interviewer:

Interviewee

G) Outdoor Observations
Seated in a Garden: Sitting, Looking and Listening.

1. Listen to the silence. Describe any emotions in you this evokes.

2. Listen and record the sounds that break the silence: birds, animals, wind, ocean, rain, people, machinery, traffic and more.

3. Emanating from the stimuli and perceptions you receive while sitting in a garden, create a poem or song, or a story or a painting incorporating these sensory impressions. You can choose to do one or more of these.

H) While Walking in a Garden...

1. Listen to the silence and take note of any emotions the silence evokes in you?

2. Listen and record the sounds that break the silence: birds, animals, people, machinery, traffic and more.

    i. Listen for barely audible sounds.

    ii. Listen to the sounds of your body in motion.

    iii. Listen to the sounds of the environment in motion.

    iv. Do you hear leaves rustling?

    v. The sounds of cars?

vi. Birds?

vii. Dogs?

viii. Cats?

ix. What else do you hear?

x. Create a poem or song about walking in your or any garden.

xi. How about a sketch or a painting?

Activity 5:
Dreams

Put on your Fantasy Goggles and…

leave the World of Reality Behind.
Enter the Vast Unknown: Your Dream World and your Imagination.

©Ellen Palestrant 2016/18

Midnight Sleep
Sometimes…
Without rhyme or reason,
Ideas dive
And
Leap
From the shelves in my dream-room
Into my midnight sleep.

From I TOUCHED A STAR IN MY DREAM LAST NIGHT © *Ellen Palestrant 2015*

©Ellen Palestrant 2016/18

At night we leave our waking world and enter one of dreams. We enter a world in which we are the creators, and the dreamscape is of us. Our dreams occur spontaneously. They are fed by reality and combined with the unconscious, linked perhaps to some great store of accumulated knowledge of which we are barely aware. In our dreams, we surrender and connect with subterranean emotions and energies that have come from—somewhere.

In dreams, our private selves escape from public demands. During the day, we drift in and out of daydreams, keeping one eye on reveries and one eye on our world. Unfortunately, we pay insufficient attention to these dreams. We have been taught not to be dreamers because realism is synonymous with maturity and an organized, responsible life.

Your Dreams

a) Dreams feed you. Do you ever get creative ideas from your dreams? List some and/or elaborate on one.

b) Do you still feel connected to your childhood dreams about what you would become one day? Elaborate.

c) How severed are you from your dreams (on a scale of 1-10)? 1 2 3 4 5 6 7 8 9 10

More About Your Dreams

I have an idea;
I'll put it to bed.

Wake up in the morning
With a story in my head.

©Ellen Palestrant 2016/18

Did You Wake up from a Sleep with a Story or an Idea in your Head?

Please Elaborate.

Write about it and/or sketch it—or capture another dream you might once have had:

Activity 6:

Activities to Develop Your Imagination and Creative Potential
(ALONE AND COLLABORATIVELY)

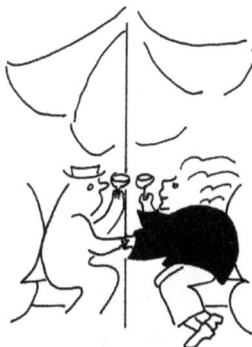

From HAVE YOU EVER HAD A HUNCH? ©Ellen Palestrant 2016/18

Food for Thought
One fresh Hunch
Two Cups of Intelligence
Two Cups of Talent
Three Cups of Daring
Four Cups of Expertise

Active ingredients:
imagination, persistence,
commitment, purpose,
enthusiasm, humor.

Stir the above together and allow it to
simmer for the rest of your life.
Don't forget to add a dash of luck

Imaginings:

©Ellen Palestrant 2016/18

Your hunch crunchers have been addressed, obstacles identified and many have faded away. They will not pounce on you again unless you let them. It is now time to enjoy that exciting meeting with the something that dwells inside you. You are ready to dip into that invaluable resource: your potential.

Imaginings:
THE MANY SIDES OF THINGS:
The Potentiality of Everything.

Nature:

Take a Tree…

It's *Botany…Art…History…Setting…Fantasy…MYSTERY*

It is a springboard to your **CREATIVITY**.

EXTENDING YOUR CREATIVITY:
DESCRIBE, DRAW, PAINT OR MODEL WHAT YOU TAKE FOR
GRANTED.
You might decide to do all of the above and add some music, too.

1. BEGIN with a tree—a visible or imaginary one.

2. Start with a leaf, a branch, the roots, the draped vines, a glistening spider web, a nest—whatever comes to you spontaneously in an outdoor setting and let *Other Sides* of the tree unfold into…Story…Poetry…Art…or a combination of all .

3. Do not censure yourself prematurely. Do not limit the possibilities that might unfold from a tree of extraordinary beauty or from one with no remarkable attributes whatsoever—or so you first thought. Using your imagination, inject the mundane with new properties. Give it an interior.

More Imaginings:

Now *Take a Mountain*

A Stream

A Puddle

or

More Imaginings:

An Inside Setting:

A House

A Door

A hard-boiled, fried, or scrambled Egg...

A Chair

A Hat

Much More.... and find

their MANY SIDES.

More Imaginings:

Can you bag one idea,

(*jot it down within the net*)

and run with it

©Ellen Palestrant 2016/18

until you find…

A Home for It?

I can never leave an idea alone.

Have to find a home for it.

If a painting isn't right, maybe there's a poem for it.

©Ellen Palestrant 2016/18

Describe or sketch your idea and also the home you have found for it:

More Imaginings:

The Possibility Boutique

I lost an opportunity.

Couldn't find it anywhere.

Looked inside my notebooks;

it had fled into the air.

Should always write my thoughts down

in case they lead to more.

Must never let an opportunity

slip through an open door.

More Imaginings:

I found my lost opportunity (It took almost a week)

under a pile of "what-if's" in the POSSIBILITY BOUTIQUE.

©Ellen Palestrant 2016/18

As I wondered at its meaning,

my thoughts began to soar.

Then I wrote a story.

Now....

There are many more!

More Imaginings:

Jot down and/or sketch your
many ideas or potential stories!

More Imaginings:

The Marsupium

From I Touched a Star in My Dream Last Night ©Ellen Palestrant 2016/18

What I would like to do

is draw a kangaroo.

Its tail would take an hour.

Its marsupium—**forty-two!**

©Ellen Palestrant 2016/18

I would design a splendid pouch

featuring a squishy couch,

a desk with drawers,

shelves with books,

shiny floors,

cozy nooks.

An ottoman,

a vased bouquet,

a Van Gogh nicely on display.

More Imaginings:

©Ellen Palestrant 2016/18

But I need a thousand hours

to draw a kangaroo!

Marsupiums are too intricate—

I'll try a cockatoo.

©Ellen Palestrant 2016/18

More Imaginings:

Do you want to draw a cockatoo

Or something…

entirely new?

Do a quickly sketch below…

Activity 7:

Unexpected Connections:
Looking at the *Known Differently*.

©Ellen Palestrant 2016/18

Connectivity

Connectivity

Knowledge without intuition is dead. It is simply details—unconnected bits. Yet, creativity is about connectivity. Once the creative urge goes beyond the hunch, the creative person resorts to many active mental processes and finds unexpected connections. That person has the ability to create new ideas by combining previous experiences with each other, or simply with imagination, that is, with what has yet to be experienced, or with what might never be experienced. Such a person, perceives resemblances between sometimes disparate things…and connects them.

If we allow information to exist untouched by our *hunches*, we simply have details, and this does not contribute to creativity. If we do not connect these details thoughtfully, instinctively and intelligently, we simply have a collection of somewhat meaningless trivia that directs nobody anywhere further. We need to perceive the similarities among things and the differences, and know that if something is similar, it does not necessarily mean it is identical.

Creative people have an ability to make rapid and unexpected connections that have a logic to them—however novel. Your instincts will tell you which combinations are appropriate and which are not. *FOLLOW YOUR HUNCH…*

Connectvity
SOME SPRINGBOARDS FOR YOUR CREATIVITY:

Some examples for you to develop further (stories, poems, art, songs, jokes, et cetera) or you can redefine them, or create your own combinations:

ABUNDANCE—a chorus line of buns in a bakery.

ALARM—a lamb's arm.

ARMATURE—a grown-up arm.

ARTICULATE—the propensity you have of arriving in the Artic too late.

BABYHOOD—not quite as dangerous as an adult one.

BACTERIA—recovered memory that elicits hysteria.

BALDERDASH—annual competition to see who has lost the most hair that year.

CARTEL—never trust a motor vehicle with your secrets.

CATALOGUE—you can order cats these days from a catalogue or catalyst.

EFFLUENT—ability to pronounce "f's" fluently.

Your turn now....

Activity 8:
My Creative Space

©Ellen Palestrant 2016/18

Creative Space

There might be a place inside your head where ideas dwell, but having nowhere to bring these to fruition, is a cruncher. Most creative people need a space, however small, to be their own and to use in their own way. Many people don't have this because of persistent realities such as financial ones that often mean too many people share the same space.

A home might have many inhabitants, each with their own needs. It becomes difficult for people in such situations to find a corner in which to be alone. Even if they find the physical space, the sounds of others continually break their solitude. Sometimes, the physical space is owned by others and therefore under someone else's control. Sometimes, even their emotional space is invaded. In an environment that is hostile or excessively regulated, it is difficult to be creative.

The space in which we create, needs to be conducive to our productivity. Some people need sunshine. Warmth and brightness enhance their creativity. Others prefer cool weather. A person can waste creative energy, however, searching for that perfect climate, that perfect place or that perfect solitude. Compromise is necessary. In terms of space, something very modest might do, simply a corner of a table in a kitchen or a worktop in a shed. Earplugs might help. Whatever you choose or have to settle for, you can only hope that it will complement you. More important than finding that ideal space, is finding what is inside your head and following your hunches. More important than the ideal space, is spending time alone with yourself.

Creative Space

1. Draw a plan of (or describe) your *current* workspace.

Creative Space

2. Draw or describe your **ideal** workspace:

Creative Space

3. Draw (or describe) a space *that **will do** because more important than finding the ideal space is finding what is inside your head, understanding your emotions and following your hunches:*

Activity 9:
Twenty-Four Hours

©Ellen Palestrant 2016/18

My Mark

Twenty-Four Hours: My Mark

Day-Not-Long-Enuffis

From I TOUCHED A STAR IN MY DREAM LAST NIGHT ©Ellen Palestrant 2016/18

Are you Suffering from

Day-not-long-enuffis?

©Ellen Palestrant 2016/18

Acute Not-catching-up-is?

©Ellen Palestrant 2016/18

Twenty-Four Hours: My Mark

A touch of Giving-up- 👁 -tis or a dose of Why-bother- 👁 -tis?

©Ellen Palestrant 2016/18

Then call

The NO-TIME-CRISIS!

PRESS ZERO for advisis ...

on slowing the clock. Beating its chime.

It's all so futilitis if time runs outis.

©Ellen Palestrant 2016/18

Twenty-Four Hours: My Mark

Analyze below how time (*lack of it or problems with time-management*) affects your Creative Productivity and list the changes you intend to make immediately as well as over a period of time to ensure that creating in some form or other, becomes a constant in your life.

Twenty-Four Hours: My Mark

We seem to be always so short of time, always in catch-up mode. There are so many competing alternatives with which we are continually bombarded, and this creates dilemmas of choice. For many people today, the social—and anti-social—networks have altered dramatically the meaning of genuine friendships, real achievements and values—and an understanding of who we intrinsically are and what we truly require in life as opposed to what we are told we *should* want to be and what we *should* acquire.

There are increasing demands on our time. Paperwork, the media, computers, the Internet, Email, social media, telephone calls, needy people, financial realities, family and social commitments tug at us, demanding attention. We have become so many things to so many people and have begun to function in a disconnected fashion.

Some of us might have the discipline to work, but others often do not have the discipline to let us do so. We have been forced to become intermittent pursuers of our areas of interest or passion. We need to take time to listen to ourselves and acknowledge our own needs. We are fragmented by the mechanical order of time and are therefore prevented from reaching our creative potential, and leaving something behind that we consider consequential, leaving our individual mark.

So…

Twenty-Four Hours: My Mark

TAKE AN IMAGINATIVE LEAP:

Let us suspend our disbelief for the purposes of this exercise and imagine that we have been given ***Twenty-Four Hours of Ultimate Possibilities…***

Twenty-four hours outside of time in which we **can** complete a lifetime of creative work.

Twenty-four hours without family, social or work responsibilities.

Twenty-four hours in which we can complete what we have always yearned to do and reach our creative potential.

Remember, this is a fantasy, so don't be modest.

If it's a perfectly planned city you wish to build, it is possible.
A park
A garden
A mural
A sculpture
A bridge,
A 1000 page novel,
The perfect poem,

It's achievable. Nothing stands in your way. So what is…

My Mark

The Mark you wish to leave behind? Write, draw or create it in any way that is meaningful to you…

Activity 10:
Collaborative Creativity

©Ellen Palestrant 2016/18

Our Mark—Creatopia

©Ellen Palestrant 2016/18

Working alone is a valuable route to discovering our creativity, and so is working with others. Even though creativity is largely a solitary process, collaborating with others helps us build up our store of criteria for something to be worthwhile. It gives us other opinions about art, science, politics, global issues, our own ideas and our own work. This can be timely and useful—as long as we have a commitment to our vision which enables us to select the suggestions which advance what we are doing, and reject those which do not. By working with others whose work and thoughts have value, we soon learn to recognize quality in ourselves and in others, and expect it.

Most creative people's work-lives consist of concurrently working independently and together. They usually give their collaborative projects priority because others depend on their contribution and could be delayed if they are tardy. Most creative people enjoy working alone, and many enjoy working alone and together.

Working with others, therefore, counteracts and complements the solitariness of working alone. Experiencing working creatively with others, is a particularly important life and career preparation. Today, collaborations of all kinds are in progress. Indeed, creativity is flowing in all directions, blending the arts with the sciences and technology, and forming new creative, multitudinous and multinational wholes. We now see the unique works of many.

Our Mark:

Creatopia—The City for and by Creators

PARTICIPANTS:
Two to twenty or more...from disparate disciplines.

Some of the people who collaborate in this exercise are not traditionally regarded as creative. They are needed because their knowledge and their insights help develop new forms: *THE MARK OF MANY:*

Design the city (plans, sketches, models, stories, songs etc.) and you might want to take into account some of the suggestions listed in the following pages. Be as imaginative and fantastical as you like. There are opportunities to create stories and theater in this exercise:

List the Names and Professions of Participants:

Creatopia—Our Mark

ARCHITECTURE

PARKS

Creatopia—Our Mark

BOTANICAL GARDENS

COFFEE HOUSES

Creatopia—Our Mark

RESTAURANTS

LIBRARIES

Creatopia—Our Mark

MUSEUMS

ART GALLERIES

Creatopia—Our Mark

PUBLIC ART

THEATERS

Creatopia—Our Mark

NEIGHBORHOODS

PUBLIC TRANSPORTATION

SCHOOLS

THE INHABITANTS

Creatopia—Our Mark

CRIME PREVENTION

ADD TO LIST

Activity 11:
Creativity Is Your Companion For Life...
Keep It Well-Tuned to Spark Your Creative Agility

A) Rhyme 1st line from words below

Create ***Two Sentences*** that Rhyme—as many as you can from this ***Word-Jumble***. You might then want to create longer verse and/or find your own words that rhyme and create verse.

An Individual or Group Activity:

Example :
One day I crashed my limousine
While munching on a nectarine...

*ABC ** batch ** patrol ** chateaus ** between ** bumble bee ** wine and dine wine ** nectarine ** carefree ** provoke ** dispatch ** chiropractor ** modifying ** contemplate ** patch ** gratifying ** actor ** ** attitude ** hobnob ** cruise-line ** cob ** category ** chateaus ** thwart ** butterflies ** modifying ** choose ** advertise ** satisfy ** gasoline ** design ** debris ** intertwine ** keyhole ** deep-sea **food ** reviewed ** submarine ** shampooed ** glows **flying ** goes ** capsize ** dominoes ** short **flows ** extractor ** primrose ** knee ** relying ** frying ** three ** applying ** limousine ** buying ** grip ** roly-poly ** guardianship ** clockwise ** cup ** ownership ** dip ** prose ** quip ** spoke ** territory ** surprise ** joke **country folk ** baroque ** lullaby ** bowl ** throb ** artichoke ** late ** guacamole ** auditory ** Aberdeen ** pantomime ** cultivate ** congratulatory ** tractor** enterprise ** Gemini ** wait ** caffeine ** cameos ** stroll ** queen ** dignify ** machine ** sweep ** storyline ** keep ** Argentine ** asleep ** excuse ** me ** news ** chime ** fireflies ** time ** quantum leap ** pantomime ** rhyme ** port ** enterprise ** job ** apple pie ** court ** up ** makeup ** prize ** tries ** skies ** slowly ** ravioli ** shampoos ** conclude ***

B) Begin Stories from A to Z very, very quickly:

Example:

A—An Antelope skiing on a slope slid into the water and…

B—Bridges and ridges were barely visible once the mist descended…

C—A Catamaran headed at accelerating speed for the turbulent waters…

Your turn now, remember from A to Z

A –

B –

C –

D –

E –

F –

G –

H –

I –

J –

K –

L –

M –

N –

N –

O –

P –

Q –

R –

S –

T –

U –

V –

W –

X –

Y –

Z –

C) *Once Upon* Stories As Many As You Can

Example

    Once upon a sunny day…
    Once upon a dark, cold night…
    Once upon a holiday…

Your turn now…

    Once upon a

    Once upon a

    Once upon a

    Once upon a

    Once upon a

C) Create Limericks

As many as you can and as fast as you can.
Example:

What a Pity!

I heard a bird in the city,
Warble a mellow, melodious ditty.
Said I to the bird:
That's the best song ever heard
In this cacophonous, crowded city.

Saw and Hammer

There was a man from Alabama,
Who ate his stew with a saw and hammer…

(For you to complete and then create many more)

D) Create Tongue-Twisters

Have Fun with Words

Do you know this tongue-twister?

Betty Botter

Betty Botter bought a bit of butter.
The butter Betty Botter bought was a bit bitter
And made her batter bitter.
But a bit of better butter makes better batter.
So Betty Botter bought a bit of better butter
Making Betty Botter's bitter batter better.
Betty Botter was written by
American writer and poet Carolyn Wells (1862 – 1942)

Now you try to create a one-line tongue-twister and then you might want to go on to do more.

Tongue-Twisters for You to Complete:

1. This Thursday, the thirty thorny, thicket thistles thrashed in the threatening thunder storm, throwing…

2. Blue blinkers blemished the blissful….

3. Crusty, crunchy…

4. What, where, whether, when will the warbler…

5. Drink drops dripping from…

Activity 12:
Glimpses of Possibility

Blog 'Glimpses Keep Falling on my Head' May 23, 2017, http//EllenPalestrant.com

Glimpses Keep Falling On My Head

Glimpses keep falling on my head and I pay attention to them because they often take me on unexpected creative journeys. Unlike the "guy whose feet are too big for his bed" *in Hal David and Burt Bacharach's song, these* "raindrops... falling on my head" do fit. So I let them *"keep falling and falling."* I never know what any of these *falling glimpses might become—and you, too, never know just what they might become.*

Glimpses or fleeting flashes of possibilities—hunches—are invaluable intuitive moments that can lead to discovery and creativity. They often seem to come out of nowhere, but many in fact, arise from past experiences, memories and image traces. May they "keep falling and falling." And may they fall on your heads, too.

Let's Glimpse!

View the painting below and see how many potential ones you can see within it. Have fun with your imagination. What do you see—Eyes, Faces, a Ladder to Eternity? Well, maybe…

2. How many potential paintings do you see in this one when you look to the left of the painting, to the right, the top, the bottom, sideways, and upside down?

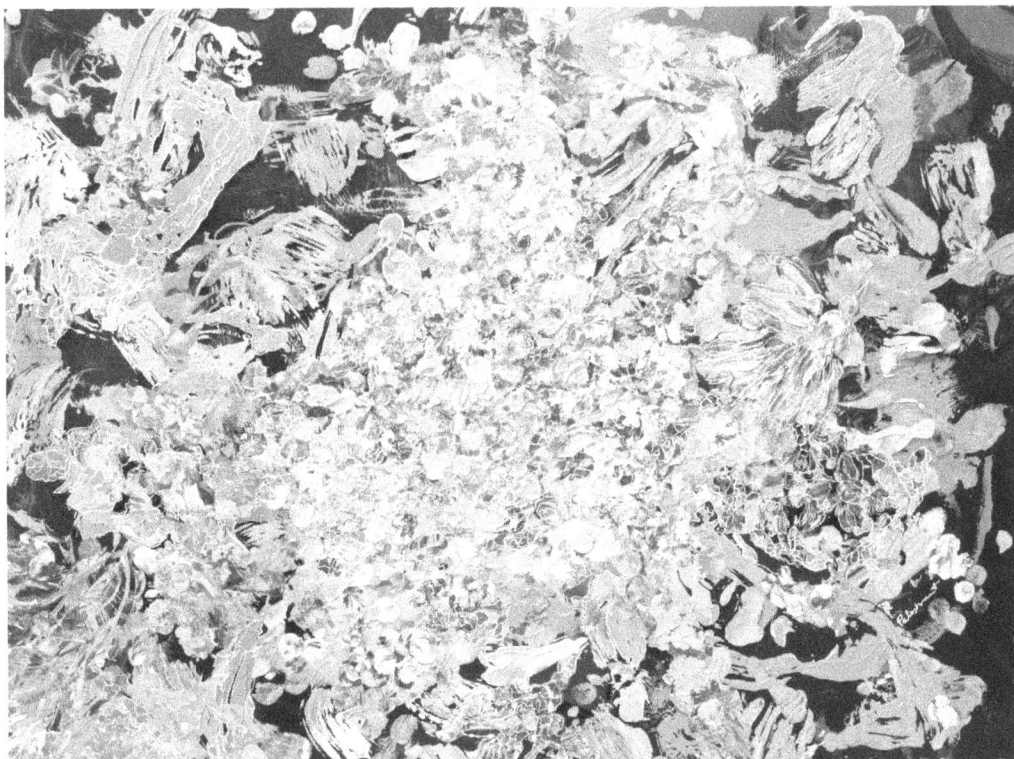

As an example, look to the left of the painting and write down what you see.

From right, middle section of the painting, what do you see? Write it down or color it in.

3. Try doing this with other paintings you view and also paintings you create. Discover many potential paintings within one painting by looking to the right, the top, the bottom, sideways, and upside down.

More Paintings within a Painting for you to Discover…

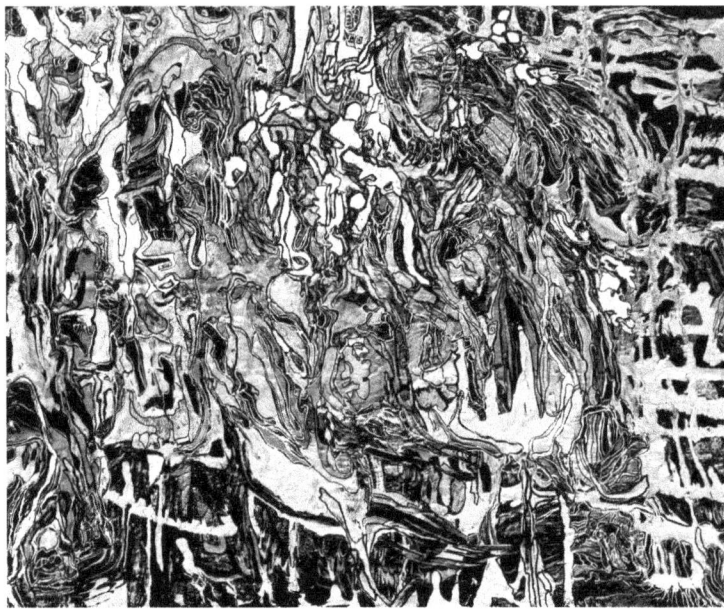

3. **Doodling is fun.** Try it with your eyes closed. Cover an entire page with your scribbles and see if anything emerges from it that you can develop into something more…

Activity 13:
Time to Reassess Yourself and Your Creativity:

Who Am I?

Who Am I?

There's me the intellectual.
Me the intuitive.

Me the apoplectical.

Me the subdue-itive.

Me the truth-seeker.
Me the phony.

Me the born-leader.
Me the lonely.
Me who hogs the spotlight.
Me who's painfully shy.
Me who is always right.

Who am I?

©Ellen Palestrant 2016/18

Who are You?

It is hard to really know ourselves. We meet aspects of ourselves in our night dreams and daydreams, but many of us are not really aware of this or that we are more than one self. We are many selves, the ones molded for public consumption and the other yearning-to-be self, almost snuffed out, barely inhaling its own selfhood, smothered by the expectations of others and of ourselves.

My Many Selves

Circle the Many Selves contained within that complex creation: *YOU. Take note of the contradictions in your make-up, and how different situations influence the self you present:*

Fragile ** resilient ** changeable ** stable ** creative ** imitative ** agreeable ** mature ** naïve ** sociable ** reclusive ** argumentative ** brilliant ** dumb ** mediocre ** emphatic ** assertive ** compliant ** constrained ** theatrical ** neutral ** passionate ** passive ** active ** dogmatic ** compliant ** constrained ** limited** unlimited ** careful ** spontaneous ** daring ** adventurous ** timid ** dynamic ** ineffectual ** competent ** inept ** judgmental ** tolerant ** provocative ** generous ** mean ** magnanimous ** organized ** disorganized ** constant ** diversified ** specific ** general ** non-conformist ** conventional ** fastidious ** careless ** casual ** formal ** simple ** extravagant ** humorous ** serious ** witty ** uninspired ** malleable ** rigid ** cheerful ** unamused ** content ** restless ** liberated ** restrained ** clear ** befuddled ** obedient **rebellious ** successful ** ineffectual **peaceful ** hostile **co-operative ** defiant ** directed **aimless ** loving ** indifferent ** motivated ** apathetic ** productive ** inefficient ** self-sufficient ** needy ** influential ** exuberant ** lifeless ** sharp ** slow ** resolute ** indecisive ** impulsive ** cautious ** visible ** invisible ** attentive ** distracted ** credible ** a charlatan ** loquacious ** taciturn ** curious ** incurious **

Activity 14:
Concepts About Creativity for You to Ponder:

A Springboard for Introspection & for Shared Group Discussion.

After thinking about the following concepts, add those which resonate with you and those to which you aspire, to the Wall of Creativity.

Abilities

Creative people draw upon many of their innate abilities when bringing their ideas to fruition. They select, combine and redesign when fulfilling their creative visions.

◇◇◇

Absolutes

Creative people are confronted with ambiguity and unanswered questions. They do not require absolutes or buy into prescribed modes of thinking—or creating—as they search for their own answers.

◇◇◇

Abstract

Creative minds can get to the heart of the matter—the idea or concept—without needing, initially, concrete, evidential support. The abstract idea resonates first and then the supporting research proceeds. They can abstract the essence of a meaning. With abstract art, the essence of emotional underpinning comes from shapes, colors, and forms that invite viewers to do their own interpretation of the artwork.

◇◇◇

Action versus Inaction

The Importance of acting, doing, undertaking and exerting effort. What is the meaning of action to you? Do you take action and how timely is your action? As artist Pablo Picasso observed, "Action is the foundational key to all success". Philosopher and writer, Antoine de Saint-Exupery said, "The time for action is now; it's never too late to do something.

◇◇◇

Adaptability

Life is not static and changes are inevitable. An adaptable person tries to understand a situation both as it was and as it has become, and then adjusts accordingly. Philosopher, writer, Holocaust survivor Viktor E. Frankl said: "When we are no longer able to change a situation—we are challenged to change ourselves". Writer Maya Angelou said, "If you don't like something, change it. If you can't change it, change yourself." Change and adaptability go hand-in-hand with creativity. When you truly are in a creative mode, you can never be stuck in old patterns of thinking.

◇ ◇ ◇

Ambiguity

Creative people are comfortable with ambiguity and do not resist it. They journey with freedom, enthusiasm and courage into the yet-to-be-known, enigmatic and hazy areas of their minds…and then into the compelling possibilities as they present. They trust that from their creative journeys, their answers will come.

◇ ◇ ◇

Appreciation

Appreciative people are conscious of and grateful for the many good things in their lives. "Next to excellence is the appreciation of it" observed writer, poet William Makepeace Thackeray. Appreciative creators value the world around them and the gift of their own ability to create. They tend not to squander it.

◇ ◇ ◇

Approaches

Creative people eagerly embrace the new. Curiosity and enthusiasm propel them onwards as they bring their creative visions into a reality. They do not regard hard work as a reason for not moving forward and exploring a project. They are finishers; they complete what they begin.

◇ ◇ ◇

Assessment

It is usually difficult to judge one's own work. Premature prejudgment can overshadow the creative individual's desire to explore even a fleeting glimpse of possibility and create it as best they can onto a form that feels just right. Self-assessment or fear of the judgment of others should not supersede the desire for creative exploration.

◇ ◇ ◇

133

Audience

Work done solely to meet the expectations of others can reduce the originality of a creative idea. Audience reactions can both benefit the creator in terms of what is learnt from a variety of responses, and it can also be detrimental in terms of reaching the potential of an individual vision. Premature self-assessment or the fear of the assessment of the others is a creativity cruncher.

〈〉〉〉

Autodidactic

Creative people are generally self-starters, self-taught and voluntarily self-challenging.

〈〉〉〉

Barriers

Judgment, condemnation, societal strangleholds are among the obstacles to creative fulfillment that some people unfortunately face. Although, their desire to create often transcends these barriers, sometimes, when entire routes to their creative futures are denied, they have to give up. Sadly, much is then lost not only for themselves, but for society as a whole.

〈〉〉〉

Brainstorming

Many minds freely sharing thoughts, innovating and building together, can give birth to greater creative wholes. The group energy from brainstorming can add to the excitement of idea generation. Some creators however, prefer to brainstorm on their own.

〈〉〉〉

Bravery

It certainly takes courage to create and plunge into deep, swirling, unknown waters and perhaps, face criticism for one's created product. It takes courage to be prepared to make mistakes, learn from them and move forward.

〈〉〉〉

Career Change

Resistance to career change can be an impediment to growth. Life is seldom static (see "Adaptability")

◇◇◇

Cheerfulness

How nice it is to spend time with cheerful people! Not only do people gravitate towards good-humored, optimistic individuals, so do creative ideas because of their receptivity and openness to the new.

◇◇◇

Childhood

The years from infancy to adolescence are a time for discovery, for freedom and for play. It is also a time for a great deal of cognitive development. Creative adults generally have an ability to combine their adult perspective with a child-like vision.

◇◇◇

Coercion

Threats, pressure, intimidation and physical force are some of the means used to control others. As opposed to freedom, these negatives have a deleterious affect on creativity.

◇◇◇

Collaboration

Collaborative work can be challenging and satisfying, and it can lead to the development of exciting projects that one person alone, could not do. "Many minds make light work as long as these minds belong to intelligent, independent and creative thinkers." (Have you ever had a Hunch? The Importance of Creative Thinking by Ellen Palestrant.©1994,2005,2014)

◇◇◇

Competition

Competition, though often an incentive to begin and try hard, can also lead to sameness because the incentive isn't to follow one's own creative instincts, but instead, to follow the products of others perceived as successful'

◇◇◇

Commitment

To follow through on a promise to complete something is a commitment. Sometimes it is a commitment to oneself, sometimes to others, and sometimes to both oneself and others.

◇◇◇

Communication

It starts with self-communication—honest dialogue with one's self. Then it is the effective, credible, way of communicating ideas to others and to the anticipated users of the product or to an anticipated audience. Good communicators are gifted sharers of ideas.

◇◇◇

Conformity

Sameness, homogenized thinking and unexamined thinking or a lack of intrinsically -generated ideas, lead to a conformity of ideas and uninspired creative productions—the antithesis of true creativity.

◇◇◇

Curiosity

A driving force in creativity: just what will the idea, the painting, the scientific hunch become? All this incorporates knowledge assimilation, much trial and error—and lots of hard work.

◇◇◇

Daydreams

"Dreams need not only occur when we are asleep. They also can be created in our conscious mind. These might be dreams of what we want for the future, expressions of deep desires and aspirations. These daydreams, these uncensored fantasies, are our rehearsals for life. Many of the choices we make can be based on them. In daydreams we audition: for the job interview, for important discussions, for roles in alternate lives. We audition in private, unafraid of the judgment of others, of being told to "get real." We are fed by our daydreams, and, if we pay attention to them, we will learn more about our yearnings. We will recognize the private, unverbalized areas within us." (Have you ever had a Hunch? The Importance of Creative Thinking by Ellen Palestrant.©1994,2005,2014)

◇◇◇

Decisiveness

Are you a procrastinator or a vacillator? Being decisive is an essential personality quality for a person who wishes that their idea or ideas will bare fruit. "Indecision can be more stressful than decision. Self-actualizing people make decisions and strive constantly to realize their goals and hence their potential, rather than hide behind indecision. There comes a time when research has to stop and we have to commit."(Have you ever had a Hunch? The Importance of Creative Thinking by Ellen Palestrant.©1994,2005,2014)

◇◇◇

Embracing Opportunities

When a new idea presents itself, do you allow yourself to explore that possibility with a curious, what-if, or I-can-do attitude instead of giving it a negative dismissal?

◇◇◇

Domain

Creative people over a period of their lives, enter new creative domains or areas of expression, expertise and knowledge. Compelled by curiosity, a need to constantly up the ante, they continually move forward—not always easy for them but often exciting.

◇◇◇

Education

Do you have a thirst for knowledge? As Italian sculptor, artist and architect Michelangelo (1475-1564) said: "I am still learning." It is important to continue to learn and grow throughout your life, however much expertise you have accumulated in doing what you do. "Education is learning what you didn't know you didn't know." (Daniel J. Boorstin, 1914-2004 - American historian, lawyer and writer). And that is what the creative life is all about—learning new techniques, acquiring additional knowledge in the service of advancing the individual journey of creativity.

◇◇◇

Effort

Consistent effort and will-power are essential ingredients in creativity. As philosopher, writer, poet and naturalist Henry David Thoreau said, "I know of no more encouraging fact than the unquestionable ability of man to elevate his life by a conscious endeavor." (1817-1862)

◇◇◇

Empathy

"Empathy is an ability that some people have to project themselves imaginatively into the heads of others and understand emotions, problems, fears and desires, that, although not their own, either could be or could never be. People can be quite different to the individuals with whom they empathize, but, because judgment does not interfere and imagination is present, they are easily able to step into those individual's shoes." (Have you ever had a Hunch? The Importance of Creative Thinking by Ellen Palestrant. ©1994,2005,2014). You need the ability to emphasize with the characters about whom you write—the social circumstances of the audiences for whom you perform—walk in their shoes even though the character might be invented the character or you might live in circumstances different to that of the audience.

◇◇◇

Enthusiasm

Are you excited about doing untried things and do you then eagerly attempt to realize the full potential of a new idea? "Enthusiasm is a great hill-climber." Said Elbert Hubbard (1865-1915)—philosopher, artist, publisher. Enthusiasm, an essential ingredient in creativity, propels you ever onward.

◇◇◇

Fear

"Fear is realistic. Imaginative, intelligent people fear danger, harm and evil. They naturally protect themselves and others—if they can—against gun-wielding maniacs, financial insecurity, loneliness, corruption, blackmail, illness and death." (Have you ever had a Hunch? The Importance of Creative Thinking by Ellen Palestrant.©1994, 2005, 2014) Are you able to sideline your fears when focused on what you are creating, fears of failure, for example, being judged or exposed as inadequate, and so on?

◇◇◇

Flow

That hazy, fascinating state of consciousness, almost outside the bounds of human cognition is experienced with ease by creative people who can enter that "one-with-the-moment zone", with great facility. In this realm of focused concentration, external distractions become side-lined and work performance is at a peak.

◇◇◇

Generosity

Are you a giver—of your time, your work, your help, your advice? Taking pleasure in giving to others and building to make the world a better place, is part of the creative process. "There are those who give with joy, and that joy is their reward." Kahlil Gibran (1883 – 1931)—Lebanese-American poet, artist and philosopher. According to American author, poet and philosopher Henry David Thoreau, "Goodness is the only investment that never fails." (1817 – 1862)

◇◇◇

Good Values

Many people have good values such as compassion, empathy, respect, trustworthiness, loyalty, dedication, self-discipline, tolerance, generosity, kindness, perseverance, and productivity. "The value of a man should be seen in what he gives and not in what he is able to receive." (Albert Einstein, Nobel Prize winner theoretical physicist—1879-1955). This can be apparent in the generosity of individuals happy to share their creative experiences with others who too, have embarked on similar journeys. Creating is about giving and Generosity is indeed, a good value.

◇ ◇ ◇

Gratitude

There is much we can be thankful for in life. There is much we can appreciate while at the same time, acknowledge our own difficulties and the difficulties and suffering of so many people.

Got no check books, got no banks,
Still I'd like to express my thanks —
I got the sun in the mornin'
And the moon at night.

Irvin Berlin (1888- 1989) "I Got the Sun in the Morning" (song)

◇ ◇ ◇

Groups

Do you enjoy working with groups?
The creative output of groups is fed when their collective energy is positive. It can be fun, energizing and stimulating when working with groups who do not have negative or competitive individuals in their midsts.

◇ ◇ ◇

Habit

Creative work habits of persistence, receptivity to the new, curiosity and diligence are examples of some of the ingredients required for leading a productive creative life. These are made all the more effective when accompanied by attitudes of enthusiasm, openness to the new and joy.

◇ ◇ ◇

Happiness

Marcus Aurelius (full name—Marcus Aurelius Antoninus Augustus) who lived nearly 200 years ago (121 – 180 AD) was a Roman Emperor and Philosopher, He said, "The happiness of your life depends upon the quality of your thoughts."

Like blind American author, activist, and lecturer Hellen Keller said: "Many persons have a wrong idea of what constitutes true happiness. It is not attained through self-gratification but through fidelity to a worthy purpose." (1880-1968). Most creative people are purposeful and it is through their work that they both enter and attain a state of calm, peaceful and happy productivity.

◇◇◇

Honesty

Honesty reigns supreme in true creativity. Characters, though invented, have to be believable, the writer credible, the painter, sculptor, musician, have to come from a place of honesty if their relevance is to endure. And importantly, the creators have to be honest with themselves.

◇◇◇

Humility

Nobody can create anything of lasting value if they bring a know-it-all attitude into the process of creating. There is always so much to learn along the way. Vulnerability and humility means being open to the new and knowing that failure might at times occur along the way.

◇◇◇

Humor

"People with a sense of humor see things differently. They recognize the ludicrous in a situation, or the incongruous or comical, and effectively give expression to these perceptions…Humor frees us from conventional ways of thinking and allows us to experiment and make unexpected connections…Humor, like wit, is primarily intellectual in that it encompasses swift perceptions of similarities in seemingly dissimilar things. It puts situations into perspective. Being able to laugh at ourselves frees us to take risks, make mistakes and face the criticism of others. It allows us to illuminate a truth humorously and yet seriously…Humorous people are spontaneous, able to laugh not only at a joke, but without editing, instantly provide one." (Have you ever had a Hunch? The Importance of Creative Thinking by Ellen Palestrant.©1994,2005,2014

◇◇◇

Imagination

Few things are more important than imagination which functions as a compass pointing you to the route ahead, and directing you into the unfamiliar areas of your mind. An ability to envisage what could be, what hasn't yet occurred or been thought of, to create fantastical worlds, music, art and much more is a gift to be cultivated and celebrated.

◇◇◇

Imitation

Imitative people are removed from themselves and their own intuition; hence their contribution to something like an artistic production is never fresh or remarkable. Some people even imitate themselves and continue to do what they had previously done because it feels safe. After all, it has been tried and tested.

◇◇◇

Inspiration

We can draw inspiration from so much around us and also from certain people who elevate our own thinking. We can become stimulated to create in some form or another and sometimes, something seemingly small can suggest something very much bigger to us.

◇◇◇

Interests

Passionate interests can stimulate creativity. Not only does the knowledge base of people grow when they continually explore their own deep interests, but so does their creativity. Such people often become so enthralled in areas that fascinate them, that they are often compelled to animate what they have learnt into another form, be it entirely for practical use or for artistic expression.

◇◇◇

Intrinsic Motivation

Motivation, the desire to do, has to come from within and not from external directions. People who are intrinsically motivated are also voluntarily self-challenging and venture enthusiastically into unknown areas that intrigue them and see what they can create within these familiar or unfamiliar domains.

◇◇◇

Intuition

When people are intuitive, their answers can come to them before reasoning and even before they have verbalized to themselves their automatic reaction to a stimuli. It feels right, and that gut feel, that hunch, is then focused upon.

◇◇◇

Joyful

Joy is invigorating both to oneself and to others. An intensity of feeling is an important ingredient in the creative process. Work and play do complement each other, nourish each other, and overlap. Joy is invigorating and therefore stimulates new ideas. (see Happiness)

◇◇◇

Luck

Of course, preparation, attitude, focus and an ability to work really hard are the prime qualities for creative production, and then there is luck which sometimes comes one's way unexpectedly—when you are open to it. As playwright Tennessee Williams said: "Luck is believing you're lucky."

◇◇◇

Memories

These are stimuli for countless created forms, ever-growing because memory is forever forming.

◇◇◇

Mentors

The right mentor for an individual can be life-changing. A mentor whose advice and guidance is trusted by an individual can also hold up a mirror for self-examination by the individual—and this mirror can also reflect the future roads to be taken.

◇◇◇

Novelty

(See originality)

◇◇◇

Opportunities

Opportunities are abundant—if we are open to them. "A pessimist is one who makes difficulties of his opportunities and an optimist is one who makes opportunities of his difficulties." Harry S. Truman (1884-1972) 33rd President of the USA.

◇◇◇

Optimism

"Optimism is the faith that leads to achievement. Nothing can be done without hope and confidence." These are the words of Helen Keller (1880-1968.) a blind and deaf author, political activist and lecturer. Optimism excites us to enter new arenas and embrace challenging projects. It is most certainly better than the negativity of pessimism for after all, "Something will turn up." Benjamin Disraeli (1804-1881)—British Prime Minister and writer. Think about your temperament: is it one of optimism and enthusiasm, essential for creative action and production? Do you have faith in yourself—and in others, too? When you begin a project, do you at the same time, experience an accompanying belief that you and the project will succeed?

◇ ◇ ◇

Originality

There are few entirely original ideas. It is where you take the idea that counts. The ability to act on a hunch—a sudden idea—and develop it by substantially participating in it's production, will lead to innovation of original products that are novel

◇ ◇ ◇

Passion

"Passion is an emotional trigger that propels creative people to persist in an effort. It supersedes the need for financial or social reward." (Have you ever had a Hunch? The Importance of Creative Thinking by Ellen Palestrant.©1994, 2005, 2014)

◇ ◇ ◇

Positivity

These are the qualities of positivity described by Mahatma Gandhi, Indian Nationalist and Spiritual leader (1869-1948):

> *"Keep your thoughts positive because your thoughts become your words.*
> *Keep your words positive because your words become your behavior.*
> *Keep your behavior positive because your behavior becomes your habits.*
> *Keep your habits positive because your habits become your values.*
> *Keep your values positive because your values become your destiny."*

◇◇◇

Purpose

"People with a sense of purpose and commitment have to risk putting their whole selves into their work, often with grim discipline and single-mindedness of purpose, but always…with the belief in the value of what they are hoping to achieve. These people are committed to their work. This commitment can be all-encompassing." (Have you ever had a Hunch? The Importance of Creative Thinking by Ellen Palestrant.©1994, 2005, 2014).

◇◇◇

Role Models (Real and Illusory)

"Positive role models are valuable and can provide hope, move people to emulation, and direct aspirations. Many of us are intrigued by the biographies of others with similar interests or goals. We learn from their work habits, their striving and philosophies. We feel less alone in our own struggles. Some role-models, however, are simply illusions, created, often, as brands to be marketed." (Have you ever had a Hunch? The Importance of Creative Thinking by Ellen Palestrant.©1994, 2005, 2014)

◇◇◇

Self-Reliance

It is very important to be self-reliant and realize that the one constant you can rely upon always is yourself. "The man who makes everything that leads to happiness depends upon himself, and not upon other men, has adopted the very best plan for living happily." Plato—philosopher in Classical Greece (428/427 BC – 348/347 BC)

◇◇◇

Solitude

There are people who have a fear of solitude, of being alone with them selves but for creative people, solitude allows for entry into their own imaginations and ongoing creations. "Aloneness is an important facilitator of creativity. Many images, whether clear or fleeting, occur spontaneously, and are hampered by external stimuli and are subsequently lost. Aloneness allows us a relationship with our intuition and the opportunity to give it our undivided attention." (Have you ever had a Hunch? The Importance of Creative Thinking by Ellen Palestrant.©1994,2005,2014)

Spontaneity

Joy, surprise, discovery, exploration, enthusiasm, and an ability to generate ideas rapidly are all stimulated by the spontaneous individual, one who is free spirited, unplanned and comfortable with improvisation.

◇ ◇ ◇

Trust

Trust of course can sometimes be naïve but it is also an essential ingredient in the creative process. If one is to create something, one has to trust one's own instincts, trust that it will all come to fruition, however long that might take, and have confidence in the path chosen.

◇ ◇ ◇

Voluntarily Self-Challenging

Being voluntarily self-challenging and not always waiting for others to set the challenge, is such an important part of creative production. One has to challenge oneself, however difficult and even grueling, the path ahead might be in order to complete what one is doing and also to succeed at it. It is all about being self-motivating, self-challenging and also, optimistic.

◇ ◇ ◇

Wall of Creativity

What I Aspire to Be, Personally and Creatively: From the concepts you have just read and about which you have thought, choose those that resonate with you for your *Aspirational Wall of Creativity* and fill them in:

adaptability

Creativity is an ongoing process; it keeps growing. Fill in the concepts as they apply to you now and fill in later—throughout your personal creative journey—as they begin to apply to you.

May you keep filling them in for the rest of your life!

Let's Do Hunch!™
You are ready!

©Ellen Palestrant 2016/18

Take your hunch to lunch today

and…

Tomorrow…

It might take you!

©Ellen Palestrant 2016/18

www.ingramcontent.com/pod-product-compliance
Lightning Source LLC
Chambersburg PA
CBHW081655270326
41933CB00017B/3180

* 9 7 8 0 9 9 9 8 2 4 7 2 6 *